LIVE RIGHT, TREAT EVERYBODY RIGHT, AND YOU WILL BE ALL RIGHT

The Autobiography of Carrie Della Beason Ellis

Carrie Beason Ellis
January 29, 1908 – March 30, 2009

AuthorHouse™
1663 Liberty Drive
Bloomington, IN 47403
www.authorhouse.com
Phone: 1 (800) 839-8640

Published by AuthorHouse 05/31/2018

ISBN: 978-1-5462-4420-2 (sc)
ISBN: 978-1-5462-4421-9 (e)

Library of Congress Control Number: 2018906374

Print information available on the last page.

Any people depicted in stock imagery provided by Getty Images are models,
and such images are being used for illustrative purposes only.
Certain stock imagery © Getty Images.

This book is printed on acid-free paper.

authorHOUSE®

Contents

INTRODUCTION

DIANE ELLIS

The well lived life of Carrie Della Beason Ellis. She was a remarkable person, facing obstacles but kept her faith in God and trust him to work any situation out. Carrie D. Beason Ellis - the first 101 years.

When you were in her presence and had time to listen, she had a story to tell you about her life. As a child taking on a responsibility of an adult after her mother died at the age of 48, taught to participate in history, not just witness it.

Ms. Ellis commentary on character and her secret for longevity, and facing racism.

The struggle of a black family, Ms. Ellis grandfather was white, and Vandy Ellis her husband's mother was white. Mrs. Ellis will take you on a journey to American history without boring you.

An introduction of a splendid woman of Good sense, grace and history.

LIVE RIGHT, TREAT EVERYBODY RIGHT AND YOU WILL BE ALL RIGHT.

THE EXTRAORDINARY LIFE OF CARRIE DELLA BEASON ELLIS - 101 years.

AUTOBIOGRAPHY

OF
Carrie Della Beason Ellis (101 Years Old)
Live Right, Treat Everybody Right, and You Will Be Alright

Carrie Della Beason Ellis was born January 29, 1908. In Moore, SC, to Perry Beason and Irene Wofford Beason.

Her siblings were Professor Beason born Dec. 12, 1904, Millie, born April 18, 1910, Grover... July 9, 1912, Ruther ...March 6, 1917, Deroe... April 29, 1919, John ... April 11, 1921, Daniel ... June 26, 1923, Gerry ... August 21, 1926, Lacre ... February 13, 1925.

(CHAPTER 1)

There were no hospitals at that time. All children were born at home. When it was time for mama to drop me, Dr. William came from Roebuck on his horse and buggy. Mama and Pa's horse was called George. When Mama was well, her and Pa went shopping. Mama said that I was a quiet baby, and when I started to walk, I would follow Pa around. My hair was long, down to my waist. Our father had a farm, and all of us had chores to do. We had to do whatever Pa told us to do. Pa was a man of many trades. He was one of the first cooks that fed 40 men that built The Tressler. It was located between Moore, and Switzer. He was a barber. He cut hair for both blacks and whites. He was a carpenter, butcher, killed hogs, packed ribs, and sausage, ham, souse meat, gardener. He owned land, and made molasses, cornmeal, and had plenty of food. He always shared with others. Whites gave Pa the nickname "Rich Nigger." Pa told us that we could have what the next person have. The color of your skin did not matter. Mama and Pa would always say, "Live right, Treat everybody right, and you will be alright.

A well-known Stellar Award Winner and singer by the name of Doc McKenzie and The Hi lites have recorded so many songs, and still are recording. Songs such as "Sow Good Seeds. If you sow good seeds, you'll be alright. All you have to do is to keep the faith and keep trusting God. These songs fit my character.

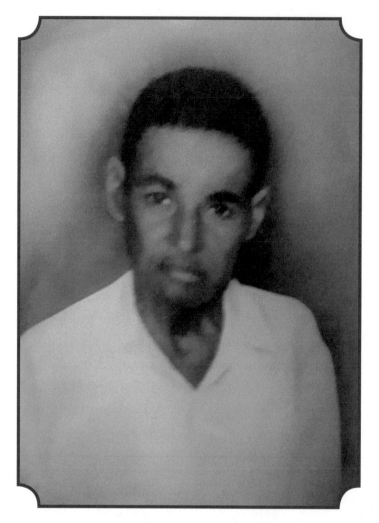

Carries Husband Vandy Ellis

World War I, known as the first war to end all wars, was a world conflict, lasting from 1914, to 1919. The war was fought by allies on one side, and the central on the other side. No previous conflict had been mobilized. This was the bloodiest war in history.

Mama's health was not good. Her favorite meat was ham. She ate so much ham that she had a stroke, and never regained consciousness. After being in the hospital for a week and three days, she died at the age of 48. Our family was devastated. Faith brought us through. Since I was the oldest sibling. I helped Pa take care of our family. My grandfather was John Henry Beason, a white man, tall, and had a deep voice. When I was six years old, I was working for white people, polishing furniture and setting out flowers. I did not have time to play "Little Sallie Walker, or pitching horse shoes with the other children. At the age of eight, I went to Sugar Ridge School. Mostly whites went to this school. My teacher was P.H. Payden and Mr. Benson. They were white. Mr. Benson and his wife lived with our family for several months. I was the smartest person in our class. Mr. Benson and his wife wanted to adopt me, and send me to school. So I could learn more, and grow up to be intelligent young lady, and get more education. They called me "Little Carrie."

Some of my friends would pay me to the "Bulk Dance. Pa went along with me being educated, but not being adopted. Mr. Benson decided he wanted to teach Algebra, when word got around, he was fired. Preaching God's word was something he liked to do. After preaching for six months, he decided to relocate.

World War II, The Global War, had the most titanic conflict in history years ago. On Sept. 1, 1939, Germany invaded Poland without warning Britain and France were at war. with Germany within a week. Australia and New Zealand, Canada and South Africa had also joined the war. Pa knew I was very smart and wanted me to be his secretary, keeping count of everything that he sold.

In the year of 1923 there were few cars. Jim Wallings who was white had a car and owned a Cotton Gin. Mace Anderson owned land. Pa and I at the age of nine 4:30 am would come down Boiling Springs Highway. It was a dirt road with top soil. It was one lane, on our horse and buggie riding until we got to downtown Spartanburg. Stopping on Trade Street, selling sausage, ham, souse meat, sweet potatoes, corn, molasses, and other vegetables. After selling on Trade Street, our next stop would be Turner's Store on Magnolia Street. Pa's check was cashed at the First National Bank. It was located up the street from Turner's Store. Our family lived in a house owned by Wolf Brannon for 28 years. He also owned a Honey Shop and sold things for horses, like horseshoes. Whatever you needed.

The Korean War from 1950 - 1953. The boundaries of the civil war through America and Russia did not clash. In that community, China fought and was armed and encouraged by Russia. The peninsula was divided after World War II back north.

The People Democratic Republic Of Korea each claimed the right, to the right to the half on the effort to unify both.

Mrs. Rouston one of the neighbors, who was white lived two house down the street. The attire back then was long cotton dresses and bunnie hats. Mrs. Rouston had big plums and a cherry tree in her yard. We would ask her for plums and cherries. She would say, get all you want and when you get them you Little Nigger children go home to your mamas. Ms. Rouston died at the age of 105. Stacks of money was found in her house.

Pa owned a saw mill. My brother John enjoyed working in the mill. He was a tall fellow. One day while working, he wasn't paying attention to what he was doing. His neck was cut off. He died instantly. Our faith got us through. All my brothers, Daniel, Ruther, Lacre, Grover, Deroe, and Gerry and Professor all married and worked in plants. When I was 16 years old I met the love of my life, Vandy Ellis. His mother was Della Jones 1879-1951 who was white. Her mother gave her away, because she had a child by a black man, and when she would go to church, she wasn't allowed to come in and worship. Word had got around. Della who was white had a child by a black man. Vandy's father was John Ellis. In 1860 he married two times to Sarah Ellis and Della Jones Ellis who had twins. The children were Louis Ellis, born December 1895, BeBE, April 1897, Dollie Ellis April 1899, Dorsey 1902, Vanerhurst 1905, Sarah 1907, Roland 1909, Connie Effie Ellis 1913, Carl 1913, Lillian 1915, Eujeane Ellis 1917. Vandy and I dated for two years. We got married, but Pa didn't give us his blessing.

He called the police on my husband, telling them that I was too young to get married. As time passed by, Pa accepted our marriage. Most of my husband's siblings live in New York City. Carl Roland, Connie and Vandy lived here in Spartanburg

Roland Ellis drove cab. Someone robbed, and killed him. The killer was never found. Connie, one of the twins travelled to New York very often to visit her sister Eujeane and Dorsey live in New York also.

At the time the Hong Kong Flu was out, and my sister-in-law caught the flu and died. Our faith got us through. While the funeral procession was passing through Spartanburg, Dunbar Street, there was a wreck. My daughter Ida was in the car that was hit. It was a rainy day. Our faith and trusting God got us through. Vandy and I was married for for three or more years. We decided to start a family. Living in Greenville, SC. My children are Pauline Ellis June 4, 1926, Ila, August 24, 1929, Dollie, Sept. 26, 1935 Earwillie, Sept. 17, 1934, Josephine May 8, 1932, Gereldine April 25, 1944, Lois Nov. 12, 1946, Roy Lee Dec. 10, 1949, I had seven girls, and two boys. My first born Pauline wanted to help me take care of her brother. One day she was being helpful with Roylee and almost dropped him, but I caught him before he fell.

Since he was a baby almost falling, fluid was around his brain. He died at one year old. While living in Greenville, SC, we attended Lone Branch Church. The church was next door to our house. I could sit in church and look out the window and see my children sleeping on the bed. Hearing God's word was very important to me. My favorite scripture was God Can Do Anything But Fail. Our family moved to Austin Street area around 1930, Spartanburg, SC. When it was a dirt road, topsoil with my seven girls and one son. They were very glad to have a brother, they spoiled him and gave him plenty of attention. In 1943, my husband started working at The Colored Hospital as an orderly. Transporting patient from one area of the hospital for whatever procedure they had to have.

I worked at Converse College for Mr. Wood, cleaning house, washing clothes. There was no washing machine. Clothes was washed in wash tubs. Mrs. Pressman another nice lady that I worked for knew I had seven girls. She would give me plenty of food for them. And while working for whites, the most of them would help me do my work. Mr. Wood would always tell me your uniforms are always pretty and white. My pay for working all week was $5.00. Mrs. Wood cut my pay to $2.00 and 50 cents. I had to find another job. My next job was working for Mr. Stein. The owner of Stein Clothing Store downtown on main street.

Josephine five years old at the time striking matches for light set our house on fire. We had to move to Hwy. 29, near Vic Bailey Car Lot dirt road, topsoil, one lane, living there for three years. We moved back to Austin Street. My husband was still working at the hospital. Segregation, white water fountain, black water fountain.

Ebenezer Baptist Church was built, I was there for the ground breaking and when the foundation was layed. The first rocks were donated. My children were members of the church. My husband's brother, Carl one of the twins, had a business selling coal, food, and other items in 1958. Our families had owning your own business in common. We decided opening our own business, calling it Ellis Cafe. Mr. Crator was the inspector.

We sold hot dogs, hamburgers, drinks, cookies, cakes, candy. After opening for two years we started selling beer. I was still trusting God. I knew that beer would make you act differently once you drunk it. Some of them were arguing with each other. I would always talk with them and calm them down. I didn't want nonone getting hurt. Each day before I opened the Cafe, I would ask the Lord to dispatch his angels in the cafe. And the Lord answered my prayers. God knew my heart. We were trying to make a living for our own family. We had a Picolo, some called it a Juke Box. Playing gospel songs and Rock in Roll. On the weekend, and through the week so much money was put in the box. The owner had to come out two or three times a week to empty the container and bring the latest songs. Tina Turner And The Consolers and other artists. My husband worked at the hospital. I had a full-time job at the cafe alone with my daughters doing whatever I asked them to do. As our business began to grow and word got around about Ellis Cafe on Austin Street. People were coming through the week and on the weekends, from the north side, the south side, east side to Ellis Cafe. Our house and the cafe was connected together. People of all ages came. Children in our neighborhood would come and get cookies and candy. Grown people getting food beer, and playing The Juke Box. Some of the men were coming there to look at my daughters and get a date.

Ebenezer Church was three or four houses down the street. Someone called The City, and complained that it was so much noise coming from the cafe. It was disturbing the church service. Several people signed a petition for us to close the cafe. We remained open. My husband died August 27, 1959. He told me that I would live longer than him. Our family was sad. We kept the faith and kept trusting God, knowing that he would bring us through. We continued to own our business.

Vietnam War 1959- April 30, 1975, was the war against the American to save the nation. There had been fighting in America for decades before the Vietnamese had suffered under French colonial rule for nearly six decades.

When Japan invaded portions of Vietnam in 1940. It was 1941 when Vietnam had two foreign powers occupying that communist Vietnam revolutionary leader to arrive back in Vietnam, of traveling for 30 years.

My daughters was so happy to have a brother, they spoiled him. When there was a fire or disturbance in the neighborhood, you could pull an alarm. It was put there for ermergencies. Some would pull the alarm just for fun, including Charles, who we call brother. The police got tired of coming. The alarm was taken out of our neighborhood.

My daughter, Earwillie was one of the lead singers on the choir at Ebenezer Baptist Church. Going to church and singing was something my daughter liked to do. Eventhough, we had a license for our business, there were illegal businesses. Such as liquor houses, and prostituting, and not paying taxes.

The street next to the cafe, Gaither Street, had several houses selling liquor and having parties. Someone would call the police. The owner would have to pay a fine or go to jail. Some were get into fights and getting cut. I continued to work in the cafe on the weekend. That's when people would come, four houses down the street was another liquor house. You could also rent a room to do whatever.

My daughter Dollie at the age of 43 died of lung cancer., in 1980. We kept the faith and knew we would be alright Josephine graduated from school and loved to travel. Going to New York City, where my husband's siblings live. Eujeane Ellis Dosey and Lillian. Ila went to New York also, to on a sleep in job. Earwillie was very quiet and got married and had six children. Ila had one child never married, and did plant work. Geraldine was married and had two children. Lois my youngest daughter worked at Ingles, the head cook, preparing food, and had one son. Pauline my oldest daughter got married and had two daughters. In 1985 the cafe burned down, to the ground. The fire Dept. said that it was faulty wires. But we learned later that it was intentionally set on fire. After that fire, empty houses in the neighborhood were set on fire. I was very sad when the cafe was burnt down. Our landlord R. T. Thompson built a house for our family, and a month later. Pa was getting older and his health was failing. He came to live with us and me and my daughters were caregivers. A hospital bed was brought out. Pa was bedridden until he passed away at the age of 84. Our faith got us through. After being the operator of Ellis Cafe for 45 years my sister Millie and I decided to travel to Ohio and Washington to visit our brothers, Daniel and Gerry.

Gerry had surgery, and a speedy recovery. We were gone for a week. I love flower gardens and pets. We had several dogs. One was named Ricky. She would have ten or more puppies, and when she was well. She would got hit by a car several times. All of us loved Ricky and wanted to keep her safe. So we took her to the country, where my sister lived in Inman. Rain was our other dog.

In 1996, a new development was built on Austin Street. It was called Ernest Rice Estates. Upper Gregory and Lower Gregory was renamed. Gilyard was renamed Carrie Ellis Court in my honor 2001, our family had been in the Austin Street community for 70 years, and we had a business. At the age of 89 I move in a new house at 278 Austin Street with my son Charles. I remain active, going to church, be there for my family, cooking, taking care of my flowers and pets. A winter storm came through mostly everyone in the neighborhood power was out. Since our family was real close, my daughters had to leave there home. And go where there was heat and lights. My oldest daughter Pauline came to my house. My lights was out. We lit candles while lighting the candles my sleeves caught on fire. My arm was burnt. The next day I was checked. I had to go to Augusta Burn Center. I was 97 years old. The rescue squad carried me there. My daughter Ila went with me there. The nurses and doctors took good care of me. They didn't believe that I was 97 years. The Lord healed me without any complications.

I continued to stay busy cooking for myself, and taking care of my dogs. Sometimes over in the night their chain would get in tangles, and they would start barking. I would go outside. It would be about 2:00am or 3:00am. I had to untangle their chain, give them food or water. When I would do that, they would be alright. My daughter Earwillie was sick and in the hospital for several weeks. When I was 99 years old my family gave me a big dinner at the church. In Inviting lots of friends. My brother came down from Washington, and Ohio and had a beautiful celebration. Earwillie had to go back in the hospital and didn't get well. She died over in the morning. Faith in God got us through. Since I was getting older my body was getting weaker. I had to go in the hospital for dehydration. At the age of 100 on my birthday January 2008 which Carrie Ellis Day recieved the proclamation from the City of Spartanburg, and a certificate from the White House..I also did a interview with Fox 21 News. When the first African American President was elected, Barack Obama, at ehe age of 100. A street was name in my honor Carrie Ellis Court. My grandmother health was failing. She had to be admitted in the hospital several times. We had to get a hospital bed. Our family members took care of her.

My grandmother always told me she didn't want to go in the nursing home. So we had to take care of her because she took care of us. She didn't suffer. Always told me that her body was so tired. Our family was her caregivers doing whatever had to be done. Bathing, and giving medicine. Eventhough she was sick, she was still joking. Told us when you get married fix your husband a big plate. I had fourteen grandchildren, four reared in the home. Irene, Diane, Candy and Shaun. Thirty-five great grand children, three great great great grandchildren, two five generations and one six. Diane my grandaughter, recorded a song with Jesus On Your Mind, and He's looking for a God fearing Man. I kept Jesus on my mind, that's how I made it through and I did fear God, knowing God was sitting high and looking low and saw everything. Diane would sing at all the funerals when a close family member would die. Her daughters Alesa and Shalonda assisting her on sometimes singing lead. During my life time I had good health. As I got older, I had high blood pressure and sinus. I stayed active. I thank God for letting me live to be 101 years old. I gave Diane permission to write this book.

Carrie Della Beason Ellis

Carrie Ellis and Family celebrating 100 Birthday

100th Birthday of Carrie Ellis

Carrie Ellis 100 Birthday Celebration

Carrie's Father
Perry Beason

Carrie's father in law
John J. Ellis

BIOGRAPHIES

DIANE ELLIS

Ms. Ellis the author of this book was born in Spartanburg, SC. Has live on the Westside, Austin Street, her entire life. She attended Highland Elementary, Carver High, and Spartanburg Technical College. She worked at Abbott Laboratory and Mack Molding Company.

In 2003, she was presented a certificate of Appreciation, and assisted in recording a Gospel CD. In 2010,, she was presented in recognition and appreciation for 40 years of faithful and dedicatied service, as a member of the Chorolettes Gospel Singers. She has two daughters, Alesa and Shalonda. Four grandsons: twins, Jermell, and Terell, George and Tye. She was inspired to write by her grandmother, Carrie Della Beason Ellis, and her mother, 90 years old Pauline Ellis Faulk. Since she had experienced so much. Singing is what she still does, and taking care of the sick.

Author
Diane Ellis on Carrie Ellis Ct

BIOGRAPHIES

VIRGINIA RUTH "JENNY" FOSTER

A FRIEND AND ASSISTANT THAT WORKED WITH AND JOURNEYED WITH THE AUTHOR Diane Ellis, during this magical time.

I attended Spartanburg High High, located in Spartanburg, SC. I graduated Summa Cum Laude in 1985, with a B.A. Degree in Social Work, and Political Science.

I've always been interested in writing and have won several literary awards, for short stories, and etc. I was employed with the Spartanburg County Dept. Of Social Services for 16 years, and retired from Spartanburg Regional Medical Center after many years.

I'm a Christian, and continue to serve my community and church as much as I can.

Jenny Ruth Foster

DEDICATED TO

Pauline Ellis Faulk
Perry Beason
Irene Wofford Beason
Professor Beason Dec. 12, 1904
Grover
Ruther
Lacre
Devoe
Daniel
John
Millie April 18, 1910
Louis Ellis Dec. 1895
BeBe Ellis April 1897
Dollie Ellis April 1899
Dorsey Ellis 1902
Vanerhurst Ellis 1905
Sarah Ellis 1907
Roland Ellis 1909
Connie Effie Ellis 1913
Carl Ellis 1913
Lillian Ellis 1915
Eujeane Ellis 1917

The Beason Family
Carrie and her Brother's and Sisiter

From left
Professor Beason born ???
Grover Beason July 9, 1912
Ruther March 6, 1917
Carrie January 29, 1908
Deroe April 29, 1919

On the right no picture
John April 11, 1921
Millie April 18, 1910
Daniel June 26, 1923
Gerry August 21, 1926
Lacre February 13, 1925

Carrie Ellis and her Brothers

Left to right: Charles Ellis, Lacre Beason, and his daughter Ila Ellis, Josephine Ellis, Daniel Beason, (Carrie D. Beason), Ellis, and Gertrude Beason

Professor Beason: Sibling of Carrie Ellis

Carrie's Husband Brother and wife
Carl and Lucy Ellis

Carrie and her sister Millie

Carrie and her daughters
Top left Pauline, Ila, Geraldine, Elwillie
Bottom left Gerdaline, Dollieruth, Louise

Carrie and her Brothers and Sister

Carrie and her daughters
Ila Ellis Josephine Ellis, Geraldine Ellis Grant, and Pauline Ellis Faulk

Carrie and her Siblings

Carrie Ellis and her eldest daughter Pauline Faulk

Gerry Beason and Friend

John Peoples Tax Service

Carries nephew
Curtis Jackson

Pauline Ellis Faulk and Marion Faulk

Carrie's daughter and husband
Pauline Faulk and Marion Faulk

Diane Ellis Barbara Jones, Beverly Moore, Beverly C. Williams, and Lee Williams

Rev. B.J. Legins and Congregation, 1941

The Ebenezer Baptist Church

Ellis Cafe

Candy and Melvin
Grand kids of Carrie and Vandy Ellis

Mother of Vandy Ellis
Della Ellis

Grand daughter Candy Ellis & great grand daughter (right)
Tyonna Ellis and (left) Tenisha Ellis of Carrie Ellis

Dock McKenzie & The Highlights Business
Lake City S.C.
Stellar Ward Winners

Carries daughter's
Josie Ellis Louise Ellis, Ila Ellis, Pauline Ellis Faulk

Carries Great Grand Shalonda Home Office working on the book

Tariah Beatty

Jermell Beatty, Alesa Wiggings, Tyrone Wiggins

Carrie's Grand Daughter
Alesa wiggins

Carries Grand children
Shalonda Ellis and Tyrone Wiggins

Carries Great Great Grand Daughter
Shalonda Ellis

Printed in the United States
By Bookmasters